Puts & Takes

Sue Edwards

BookLeaf Publishing

India | USA | UK

Made with ❤ on the BookLeaf Publishing Platform
www.bookleafpub.in
www.bookleafpub.com

Dedication

To the person who made made me a Mama and made me whole, I am forever grateful. To my person who loved me fully and unconditionally, I am forever grateful. To all the animals I have held and loved and to all those who have mapped to my soul, I am forever grateful. To the the group of beautiful souls who have helped me see the light, I am forever grateful ~ xoxo

Preface

This series of writings is of my own words and thoughts. I married my best friend and life happened. These poems are personal and my own experiences about some of that life. I have received no formal training in writing poetry and in fact, I used to have a hard time writing in general. If you knew me "way back when" you'd be very surprised to be holding this in your hands or reading this online. Life is full of puts and takes. Grateful. Thankful. Blessed.

Acknowledgements

To all those whose paths have crossed mine - there was a purpose in every step, every word, and every action ~ xoxo

1. Sweatshirt

The embrace feels like a well worn sweatshirt.
The smell, the feel, the security, the softness.
How it wraps around my body like a trusted friend.
There's a comfort of falling into something that knows
me so well.
The love, the connection, the ease.
The sweatshirt was once new, fresh and struggled to
keep up
It now knows me better than I know myself.
Knows when I need it, when to stay away, and when to
come close.
The sweatshirt is him, it has always been him.

~ xoxo

2. The Way

The way our years have been
The way his mouth curls up when he laughs
The way he glides across the top of the water
The way he floats under the sea
The way his eyes crinkle when he laughs
The way his thumb caresses my hand
The way he smirks when he looks at me
The way his eyes twinkle when our gaze meets
The way he opens the door for me
The way he puts his hand on the small of my back
The way he has taught me patience
The way he fathers his children
The way he moves when he runs
The way his legs carry him
The way he is sensitive and strong
The way he competes
The way he loves
The way he listens
The way he takes care of me
The way he loves our pets
The way he respects our differences
The way he embraces our likenesses
The way he smells of neoprene after diving
The way he head tilts when he wants me to acknowledge

something
The way he is humble
The way he greets me when I return home
The way he likes to watch football
The way he cries when he laughs too hard
The way he makes everything okay
The way he loves his family
The way he is
The way I fell in love with him.

~ xoxo

3. For You

You know before I seek.
You know before I act.
You know before I speak.
You know before I XXXXXX
You are my soulmate.

~ xoxo

4. Pain and Exhuberance

I like the pain and then I don't
I like pushing myself and pushing more
I like feeling as if I can't take another step, and then
somehow I do.
I like crying at mile 80 and then I don't
I like eating all the trails snacks and then more
I like hearing noises in the woods that don't' make me
stop in my tracks, and then somehow I do
I like feeling the pain in my back and hips then I don't
I like the secrets of the trail family and then babbling
more
I like how my body does not want to go, and then I barge
ahead more
I like experiencing hallucinations while running, and
then I don't
I like being alone on the trail and then crave the
seclusion more
I like it all, all the pain and all the exhuberance of the
trail.
~ xoxo

5. Brothers and Sisters of the Trail

The task before us was daunting, but moving forward
was the only way;
it was mile 0 of 100 and when "Go" was called, we went.
The eager looks, the excitement, the pure joy. No
contender know what lay before them, but all knew
what they left behind.
The energy surged through us and we passed it onto the
earth; in turn, she shared her beauty and allowed us to
absorb her.
As if dancing to their own music, the sun and moon cast
their shadows on the beach and in the forest; tricking
our eyes and challenging our minds.
Each hour and each loop brought a different perspective
and a new meaning; when night fell the beauty blurred.
The Pier, like an unwelcomed friend, was tough; she was
unforgiving and did not bend; she was beautiful in her
own strange way; and it's not until she saw our final
struggle that she finally relented and showed her
kindness.
Friendships were solidified and lifelong bonds made;
brothers and sisters of the trail, soul searching and
dream catching. Each rejoicing in their own victory.
Exhausted yet stronger; no words need spoken but many

tears were shed. In the end, our bodies are the same, but our hearts have forever changed.

Mile 100 of 100, we are brothers and sisters of the trail.

~ xoxo

6. Under a Blood Red Moon

The hue is red
My soul been fed

The air is clear
I have no fear

The sky is bright
Yet there is no light

The stars have tails
The run never fails

~ xoxo, 2014

7. Moon Shadows

I am drawn to you like a moth to the light;
I am drawn to you like a captain to his vessel;
I am drawn to you like a woman to her lover;
Your beauty draws me to my senses.
Your beauty draws me to my knees.
Your beauty draws me.

~ xoxo, 2013

8. The Morning Run

The light of the moon
The sight of the stars
The peaceful sound of night in the air
whispering about the day to come.
The glistening of the dew on the blades of grass
The smell of the moisture in the air
The awakening of the day
the peaceful chaos begins.
The sounds of the birds waking
The petals of flowers opening up
The lightness breaking through the sky
like slowly shattering glass.
The smell of bacon wafting through the air
The carefree laughter of children
the simplicity of early days.
The Saturday morning run.

~ xoxo - March 2015

9. The Love of the Skydive

The donning of the equipment.

The smell of the jumpsuit.

The electricity in the air.

The waiting.

The practice exit.

The time to go.

The propellers pushing the wind in your face.

The climbing the ladder onto the plane.

The click of the seat belt.

The eager faces.

The smell of excitement.

The sound of the engine.

The rattle of the door closing.

The checking of equipment.

The sounds of altimeters going off at 1,000 feet.

The unclicking of seat belts.

The enthusiasm in the air.

The grins.

The smiles.

The nervous energy.

The sounds of the tandems.

The high-fives, the lo-fives.

The sky shake.

The respect.

The safety check.
The opening of the door.
The whirling of the wind.
The sound of altitude.
The red light.
The green light.
The go.
The joy of the jump.
The freedom.
The curvature of the earth.
The line of the runway.
The different hues of blue.
The shades of green.
The depths of the clouds.
The silence.
The chaos.
The rush of activity.
The flying through the air.
The touch of a cloud.
The rays of the sun.
The reflection of the sun on the water.
The world oblivious to its own beauty.
The opening of the canopy.
The peace.
The serenity.
The euphoria.
~ xoxo

10. I've Missed It

Over the months I've had dreams of this day.
I craved the solidarity, the rhythmic breathing, the sound of my feet hitting the ground,
sounds of birds waking up, the sight of our beautiful sun greeting me in the morning.
Alone with my thoughts, alone with nature, feeding my soul.
I could feel the little parts of me awaken that had been sleeping for months.
I could feel my drug of choice hit my veins.
It was glorious and something I'll never take for granted.
I need to feel this every single day

~ xoxo

11. The Man Next to Me

The man next to me...
Is strong
Is bright
Is funny
Is my anchor.
He illuminates
He radiates
He shines
He is my light in a storm.
My best friend, my soulmate, my life partner, the father
of three wonderful children.
I have been blessed for the thousands of days and the
millions of minutes we have spent together and look
forward to the thousands and millions to come.

~ xoxo

12. Oh Black Box

You approach me from afar
I see your darkness coming but can't seem to fly far
enough away to escape you
You seduce me into thinking I should follow you
You show me solitude and silence
You bring me doubt and desire
You suffocate me
You keep me restrained with chains I cannot see, you
clip my wings
Sometimes I am able to escape
Sometimes I am able to feel
Sometimes I remember what it was like
And, sometimes I start seeing shards of light peeking
through
I start flying that way
But then you chase me again and I fly back into the
solitude of darkness
I briefly remember what it feels like to see brightness
and beauty, to see colors and hear song, to enjoy, let go
and be free
It's fleeting, but it's imprinted on my mind and it brings
me back from the darkness
Slowly I begin to shed the wings of darkness and hope I
am not lured back into the pit where I've become so

comfortable

I finally feel my wings lifting me out of the black box,
towards the laughter, trails, the sun, and the beauty I
once knew.

Slowly, steady and sovereignly

I become me again.

~ xoxo

13. Just One Week

Just last week, he signed up for a virtual 1,000 mile bike race.

Just last week, he was reciting Shakespeare sonnets by memory.

Just last week, he was diligent in his training and nutrition.

Just last week, he did not forget anything.

Just last week, he was solid.

Just last week, I was his wife.

Just last week, we were saying how perfect our lives are.

Just last week, we were talking about the trips we wanted to take.

Just this week.Just this week, he leaves doors open.

Just this week, he sleeps a lot.

Just this week, he does not remember to eat.

Just this week, he is not active.

Just this week, he forgets the dog.

Just this week, he has no routine.

Just this week, he is not predictable.

Just this week, he is unsteady.

Just this week, he is a different man.

Just this week, I am afraid to leave him alone.

Just this week, I am afraid he will never be the same.

Just this week, I love him more than he will ever know.

Just this week, I am his wife and his advocate.

Just this week, we have memories of what was.

Just one week.

~ xoxo, 2020

14. Take This Day

As my heart fills with joy
I remember it is not others, but me,
who controls my own destiny
Take this day as it is, give back, and simply be.
~ xoxo

15. The Moon

Her power
Her beauty
Her strength
Her attraction
She know none of it
She never fails
She's a beacon for lost souls
She always shows her brilliance
Her energy keeps us grounded
Her connections run deep
Her dependence is key.
~ xoxo, 2016

16. Anger and Peace

Angry at the lies.
Angry at the truth.
Angry at the betrayal.
Angry at the deception.
I shared the burden.
The anger released.
The anger dissolved.
The anger liberated.
The anger left.
Peace about the lies.
Peace about the truth.
Peace about the betrayal.
Peace about the deception.
Grateful for ignoring my pride.
~ xoxo

17. Free and Not Free

Free.
Free from the restraints we put on ourselves,
judgments, free from a schedule, meetings, mind
pollution,
appointments, driving, outside distractions,
conversations you don't want to have or conversations
you want to have,
free from expectations, free from your mind going in a
million different directions at once.
Free.

Not Free.
Not free from the beautiful trees standing tall and proud,
silence,
the leaves ready to fall and rebirth after a long winter,
or the sound of the river running to join forces
elsewhere,
the sun enjoying a night of rest so it can shine the next
day,
the smell of rain and the feeling of the rain on your face
while running.
Not Free from the smells of the forest, decaying leaves,
the sounds of coyotes in the distance, cows,
the beautiful pure darkness except for a headlamp way

off in the distance,

the amazing flying spiders, the beautifully arranged corn fields,

the orange crescent moon after the rain and its reflection in the canal,

and the bright beautiful stars - oh the beautiful, beautiful stars. .

Not Free.

~ xoxo

18. I Saw it Coming

I saw it coming
The ground was moving faster than I imagined
I saw it coming
The film of my daughter's life played in my head
I saw it coming
The colors were so vibrant and so beautiful
I saw it coming
The giggles and laughter forever etched in my mind
I saw it coming
The first bite of real food and her bright blue eyes full of
surprise
I saw it coming
The first ride on a tricycle and the mixture of fear and
joy
I saw it coming
The landing was hard and the visions stopped.
I saw it coming.

~ xoxo

19. Have You Ever

Have you ever...

Been in the middle of a forest and heard the silence of the night?

Tasted a cloud?

Cannon balled out of a perfectly good airplane?

Shared an ice cream kiss with your child?

Watched a butterfly get nectar from a flower?

Witnessed water flow over a stream so elegantly that it doesn't t lose it sheen?

Watched the sun rise and set from the same seated position?

Counted the freckles on the face of a loved one?

Listened to the raindrops falling on the leaves in the woods?

Watched the sunrise at Croom, shining brightly through the beautiful pines?

Run the ridge in a Georgia mountain?

Taken a million pictures during a 10 miles run?

Seen the curvature of the earth while floating above it?

Listened to the breath and the beat of your lovers heart all night long?

Laughed until you cried and then laughed some more?

Listened to the muck sucking the shoe off your friend's foot?

Loved someone so much that your heart aches?

Reach someone on such a deep level that it frightens you?

Been on the way to a dream and found a better one?

Snuggled your loved ones from dawn to dusk?

Listen to an animal run through the forest?

Wanted to jump out of a perfectly good airplane and touch the clouds?

Felt the electricity of the earth beneath your feet?

Flown through the sky with the greatest of ease?

Really feel the pine needles under your feet while walking in the forest?

Smell the beautiful aroma of decaying wood?

Listen to the birds awaken each morning?

Fed the homeless?

Put on a pair of running shoes and simply run as far as your heart will take you?

Watch the rays of a full moon shine behind the night clouds?

Listen to the sound of a wooden bat hitting a baseball?

Watch the waves roll over and over again while listening to the beautiful seagulls?

Noticed the the crow that visits your house often has a deformed foot?

Heard the whoosh of the plane door before you jumped?

Watched the sun and moon cast shadows on the beach?

Felt the silky moisture of a cloud on your face?

Run 200 miles?

Do It. Do It All.

~ xoxo - 2015

20. The First Sip

As the world awakens
I open my eyes and the fog slowly clears.
In the dark I make my way to the kitchen,
open the cupboard, and search for my favorite mug.
I am alone with my thoughts of my dreams and those of
the day ahead.
It's both comfortable and comforting. It's routine.
The clinking mug being placed on the counter and the
sound of the coffee filling my cup.
The smell of coffee brewing and the beeping sound when
it's done
Oh, one of the simply joys of life ~ that first sip.

~ xoxo

21. F & G

Fear.
Fear that I would not be able to watch my daughter
graduate from high school
Fear that I would not be able to teach her to drive
Fear that I would not see her 16th birthday
Fear that I would not help her decorate her college dorm
room or see her graduate from college
Fear that I would not be able to see her enjoy her life
Fear that we would not share the special moments to
come
Fear that my husband will not have a partner for life
Fear that we would not be able to do all the things we
wanted to do
Fear that I would - at the end of my life - have regrets
Fear that I was not truly living
Fear that I would not live 5 years after my diagnosis
Grateful these fears never came true
Grateful that I have been able to watch my daughter
grow and see the glint in my husband's eye
Grateful for life and the give and takes
Grateful for each breath, each experience and each
person.
Grateful.
~ xoxo

9 789363 308626